Stop Caring What Others Think

How to Stop Worrying About What People Think of You

James Umber

www.southshorepublications.com

© 2015 by SouthShore Publications & Distribution.

ISBN-13: 978-1511800419

ISBN-10: 1511800410

Claim Your Free E-book!

As a thank you for taking a look at this book I want to give you an e-book that is completely free right now! This book is not available on Amazon or anywhere else and is completely exclusive to my readers.

This book is called "Improve Your Personality – 8 Super Simple Personality Traits That Will Make People Instantly Like You"

This completely free book is so powerful because it will show you how to instantly boost your personality, which enables you to simultaneously improve your social life, your work life and your love like all in one go!

To get the free book right now, simply go to this link:

www.southshorepublications.com/improve-your-personality

The Other Books in my Book Series:

THE SECRETS OF SUCCESS &
SELF IMPROVEMENT
BOOK SERIES

Creative Visualization Techniques

Passive Income for Beginners

CONTENTS

Introduction

Can you think of a time when you have done something you know you didn't want to do, just to please other people and keep them happy? Of course you can, we all can.

Why do we let other people's opinions have so much power and control over us? Why do we let what other people say and do influence our own actions and choices?

These are the questions I am going to tackle and break down in this book. To understand this properly we need to look at the reasoning hidden behind our thought processes, both in the form of conscious thoughts and automatic subconscious paradigms.

Once I have given my thoughts on this and we understand the psychology behind the problem. I have one super simple tip that has massively helped everyone I have ever taught. It's such a simple decision and mindset that anyone can implement it in their lives from day one. There's nothing complicated about it at all. It's one of those things that when you hear it, you will not understand how you hadn't realized it before on your own, but no one does!

Whether you admit it or not most of your day to day decisions probably aren't based on what you truly want, they are based on how you think those decisions will make you look to other people.

We all do it to some extent. Some of us however are more, what I would call, "people pleasers" than others. Some people will feel such a burden to please others that they will actually make decisions that are detrimental to themselves, just to improve other people's opinions of them.

Now there's nothing wrong with doing nice things for people. The problem comes when you do these nice things because you feel like you have to for some reason or another. Or you are doing it in order to gain recognition from the person you are doing it for, not because you actually want to do it.

Some of people will be so used to pleasing other people in order to better others opinions of them, that their subconscious mind will tell them to do something when they're asked to without even thinking about the option of saying, "No, I don't want to."

They may feel like by saying no they will seem like a bad person and that someone's opinion of them may be lowered due to this.

The information I am about to give you in this short book will not only enable you to live a far more care free, happy existence but it will also set you firmly back on the path to achieving the success that you truly want and deserve out of your life.

Your Self-Image

We all have an image of ourselves in our minds. An idea of what kind of person we are, what we're like and how other people see us.

If you're the kind of person who goes out of their way to help others then you will have an image in your head of yourself being a good, kind hearted, giving person. You may be someone who wants to do good deeds and you may see yourself as someone who can make the world a better place for other people by doing things for them and making them happy.

Ideal Self-Image

People like this want others to perceive them as they see themselves in their self-image. So by doing all these kind things for other people and pleasing them they are causing people to see them as they see themselves in their mind.

The thing is, we don't just have a self-image in our minds. We have an ideal self-image. So it's not an image of what we actually are, it's an image of what we want to be and how we want others to see us.

Validation

We strive for validation from others in order to feel good in the knowledge that they see us as we see our ideal selves in our mind. We want to believe that we are our own ideal self-image and we want proof that we are just that.

This validation could come from anywhere, we don't care. It could be from someone important such as a family member or friend. It could be from a co-worker or even the guy behind the counter at your local shop. It could even be from a total stranger when you pick up something they have dropped and return it to them for example.

It takes a lot of effort to make people take enough notice to provide you with validation. Especially if your ideal self-image is set at a very high standard. But we still try and put all of this effort into being seen as the person we want to be just to get that validation that we crave.

Negative Comments

So what happens when someone says something that isn't in line with your ideal self-image? You really don't like it. Who likes to hear things that we don't want to believe about themselves? So what do you do? You start working even harder to change their opinion of you to align with how you want to be seen by other people.

So really it's our ideal self-image that is causing us to care so much about what others think of us and therefore alter our actions and our lives to make people see us how we want to be seen.

Trying to get everyone to see you how you want to be seen is not only impossible, it can also cause you a lot of stress. Especially when you're not getting the validation and recognition for your efforts that you believe you deserve.

The Selfishness of Human Nature

Human beings are selfish creatures by nature. There's nothing wrong with this, it's a basic survival instinct. If we didn't have any selfish desires our species would have died out before it even got going.

Selfishness isn't as much of a bad thing as it's made out to be. We do need to do some things that are just for us and that will benefit us solely.

Being Selfless

When you are doing selfless things for other people, it can feel really good because of the validation and praise you get from them. But if you do this too often because you are craving that validation too much, you are actually working against your instincts and your human nature.

This problem gets worse when you are constantly telling yourself that you're not a selfish person. When your self-image is of a selfless, kind person you are not only working against your nature you're actually denying it to yourself in your mind. But your human nature and your selfish instincts are still there, you're just suppressing them.

The Inner Conflict

You will find that after a while, maybe a long while, your instincts and your human nature will not just take this lying down. You will be causing an inner conflict inside yourself where your conscious mind is telling you one thing and your instincts are telling you another. Given time this will grow and grow inside you and become volatile and unhealthy.

You will probably begin to resent the people who you are doing these nice things for. You will experience anger and frustration, especially if people have begun to expect you to be this nice, giving, selfless person. They may no longer be giving you as much validation because it's just what they have come to expect of you.

Now, I'm not saying to be a completely selfish, horrible person and completely give up on your self-image. Just alter it so that it aligns more with what you really want for yourself rather than how you want to be perceived.

The Middle Ground

If there is a spectrum of paths in life consisting of people who care more than anything what people think right though to those who couldn't care less about other people, then surely the best path to take is right down the middle.

How Much To Care?

The people who care too much about what other people think will spend their lives trying to gain recognition from other people and do things for the benefit of others to get it. They will never get anywhere in life because their mind is consumed with what other people think of them and they don't have the time or energy left to consider what they really want.

The people who don't care at all what other people think will only do things for the sole benefit of themselves. They will obviously be disliked by everyone and be seen as a horrible person. The opposite of a people pleaser. No one wants to be despised and lonely and this is not what I am telling you to do. Things aren't as black and white as this.

Walk Your Own Path

You need to walk your own path right down the middle. By doing this you will follow your instincts to develop yourself and gain things that you want in life, but also still use some of your time to do nice things for others because you genuinely want to, not because you feel like you have to.

My point being that you shouldn't want to completely not care what people think about you. Other people's opinions can sometimes be helpful in life. You should just care about those opinions the appropriate amount.

So what if a few people don't like you? It doesn't matter as long as there are other people that do, they are the ones that should matter to you. Why spend time trying to convincing people who don't like you that you are such an amazing person, when you could be spending that time on your personal development and doing things that you really want to do with your life?

You can't accomplish the things you truly want to in life if you're over dependent on the opinions of other people. You need to start doing things for you.

Why Do Opinions Matter Anyway?

Ask yourself this. What is an opinion? It's just a thought that is in someone else's head. It is literally just a figment of someone's imagination.

By overly concerning yourself with someone else's opinion, you're letting a figment of someone's imagination control your actions and your emotions.

When To Listen

Now, if this opinion is formed by someone that you value the opinion of then it's probably worth listening to. I'm not telling you to completely stop listening to family and friends for example. I'm just telling you to not let those opinions change your path in life and hold you back.

But some of us will be overly effected by the opinions of people who don't even really matter to us. So these opinions that only exist in the minds of people we don't even care about are actually having such an effect on us that we change our actions and thoughts to counteract them. This is when problems arise.

I want you to really think about that for a moment. It's crazy how we let something that someone we may not even like very much has made in their head control us to this extent.

No one should have this kind of power over us, especially people we don't even care about. We should be in control of our own actions and thoughts and not let other people's opinions negatively impact our lives and keep our minds from focusing on what we truly want.

Positive Opinions

It's important to remember that it's not only negative opinions that will influence your actions and behavior. Sometimes when people form good opinions of us, it can have even more of a negative impact on us than negative opinions.

If we do something nice for someone to give off the impression that we are the kind of person in our ideal self-image, they will often respond with a positive opinion and voice that opinion to us. This provides us with positive reinforcement, which is an extremely powerful thing.

So both negative and positive opinions that other people create change and affect us massively.

Controlling Other Peoples Thoughts

Another thing to consider is what you are actually doing when you hear an opinion and you act upon it. If you hear something negative about yourself, you obviously won't like it. Most people will then set about trying to change the opinion of the person who thinks the negative things about them. So they're actually trying to control the thoughts of another person.

Trying to control someone else's mind through your own actions is quite bizarre if you think about it. Mainly because their thoughts and opinions are usually not so much a reflection of you, but rather a reflection of them and the way their mind works.

So you waste your time trying to change someone's opinion when in actual fact, that opinion is their problem, not yours.

Mood and Emotion

Another thing that places other people's opinions even further out of your control, no matter how hard you try, is mood and emotion. You have to remember that both of these things will change someone's opinion of you and even change the way that they give that opinion.

So for example, if someone is having a bad day and you then ask them for their opinion on some aspect of you or your life, chances are they will respond negatively because their emotions are interfering with their judgement. So why would this opinion matter to you? Why would you let one thing that one person said when in a negative frame of mind change your actions?

Bad Opinions

Another thing to think about is that maybe that person's opinion is just plain bad. Sometimes people will give us bad advice and bad opinions, we may still listen to them anyway because we think maybe we are the ones who are wrong.

So sometimes you will actually be changing yourself to suit someone else's bad opinion that holds no value anyway.

The point I'm trying to make is that opinions are random. They are effected by a whole number of things that are totally out of our control. Trying to control randomness is a huge waste of your time and effort as it's impossible. If you try to do this with everyone then you will spend your whole life trying to master the chaos and not get anywhere or achieve anything that you want to.

Know What You Want

Knowing what you want, what you truly want, is so important in order to stay grounded and not let other people's opinions effect you. This is the secret to not caring about what people think of you.

For example, if someone told me that they thought the fact I made books was stupid, do you think I would let that affect me? Of course not! Because I know what I want, I want to be writing books. Writing these books is a part of my life plan and there is no way I would let other people's opinions change the way I act or think about my life plan in any way.

Be Selfish

You need to become driven and self-motivated, and part of that is letting that selfish nature that I talked about earlier come through and help you find what you want out of life. Once you know what you really want, these opinions that other people have will seem so insignificant and small you will stop caring about them without even realizing it.

Visualize

Imagine your path through life as a straight line stretching out ahead of you. That path is surrounded by other people. All of these people will have opinions and thoughts and they will be coming at you from both sides.

You have to make a choice. Are you going to keep stopping on your path to listen to their opinions and act upon them? If you do you will have to halt on your path and put time and effort into altering that opinion. All the time you are doing this you aren't moving along your path and you can never get back that time and effort you have wasted. Are you really going to let people's opinions do this to you?

If you don't know what you want out of life, or what you want your path to become, then it's much easier to get distracted by the people on the sidelines.

All of these people will have their own paths that are crossing yours, be it a fleeting crossover of paths or a slightly longer crossover lasting a year or 2 years for example. Eventually, for most people, their path will leave yours. It up to you for how much of this crossover of your two paths you let them stall you for by acting upon their opinion.

The Opinions That Matter

You need to remember that you can't just never listen to what anyone thinks again. Other people's opinions can be valuable in the form of feedback. We just want to block out the unwanted opinions of people who we don't really care about who are judging us.

Filter Opinions

So to use the obvious example, an artist creates a painting. How would they grow if they didn't listen to what other people thought about their work?

Now, while this is true, it can also be hugely detrimental if he cares too much about what they think. If he gets negative feedback on a watercolour painting that he tried out when he really wants to be an oil painter, he may work on improving his watercolour skills to prove them wrong when he truly wants to be doing oil paintings. This is causing him to stop on his path when all he was intending to do was to listen to some feedback.

Criticism

It's also important to differentiate between feedback and criticism. Criticism is dangerous because if you listen to it and let it affect you then you can easily begin to doubt yourself.

How many great artists do you think were told their art is terrible and that being an artist won't earn them any money, only to go on to sell paintings for thousands? Pretty much any successful artist I would imagine at various points through their career.

The ones that fail are the ones that take the criticism and let it make them doubt themselves and change their path in life and their vision because of it.

Choose Who To Listen To

As I said though, sometimes it's good to have people around you that have a different opinion to you and give you a reality check and to make you think about what you're doing. But when you listen to these opinions, don't let them control you. If you hear a great opinion then you can take it on board.

So only listen to relevant opinions that you know are worthwhile. Only let opinions have an effect on you if they are in line with your path in life. If you are grounded enough and believe in yourself and your vision you will be able to do this easily.

This is important because if you listen to all of the opinions around you then you will end up just going round in circles. You can never please everyone, so pick and choose.

Praise and Validation

An important issue that I touched on already is that positive opinions and praise are just as dangerous as negative feedback and criticism.

Believe In Your Own Path

Going back to what I was saying about artists as an example. It's important that the artist doesn't go seeking validation and confuse that with feedback. It's nice for him to hear people telling him that his painting is fantastic of course but by doing that he may change his artistic vision to create more paintings like the ones he gets the most praise from even if he personally prefers different ones.

Don't Reply on Praise for Validaiton

If you're truly doing something for yourself and you believed in your path you wouldn't need outside validation in order to be sure of yourself.

So, if an artist did a painting and he was grounded and believed in what he was doing, then he wouldn't need other people to tell him it was good in order to be happy with it. But some people do need this validation, and it's because they don't believe fully in their own path.

It's also important to not start to reply on and get too used to praise. Sometimes you won't get any. This is when problems can really start to occur.

Even if no one is saying anything bad about your work or being overly negative. You will still be thinking about the praise you usually get and wonder why you're not getting it. This leads to self-doubt and it will cause you to be unhappy and try to work out exactly what it is you're doing wrong so that you will get the praise again next time. This is pulling you away from your path in order to, once again, try to please others.

So both negative and positive opinions are just as harmful as each other. In fact positive opinions may be more dangerous in the way that we actually want to hear them and seek them out.

Don't Expect Validation

Another problem with seeking praise is that once you begin to expect it or crave it too much, you can actually start to resent the people who aren't providing you with it.

You may start to actually become angry with people close to you because you find their lack of praise and validation to be insulting and even rude.

Or some people may even be annoyed when they are given praise because they don't feel like the praise is strong enough considering all of the effort they have put in.

All of this just serves to hold you back further. How can you be focused on following your path when you're far too concerned with waiting and expecting other people to validate your efforts? All you need to do is focus on if you're happy with your own personal progress.

Why Does it Matter?

Also, what is the true value of praise anyway? It's nice and it will make you feel good for a short while. But on the grand scheme of things it's not bringing any real tangible value to your life. What is the point in seeking out this validation constantly if it's only temporary?

Achieving your personal goals in life is what's really fulfilling. Not these compliments and opinions of other people.

Acceptance

So we need to know what we want and where we want our path to lead us, this is our focus. With focus we become grounded and are able to block out other people's opinions because we realize they don't matter as long as we are happy with our progress through life.

We also know how negative and positive opinions are harmful and that they are just thoughts created in a person's head. So it would be silly to let them have control over us in any way.

But how do we actually implement this? The first thing you need to do is accept the fact that the way your mind is working right now is detrimental to your life.

Realize the Problem

You need to come to the realization that the way you have been functioning is not working for you and accept the fact that you need to change this. This can be hard to do seeing as you have had this way of thinking and this thought process in your head for your entire life.

You need to accept that you have to let go of the way you see yourself in your head and your ideal self-image that you have had for as long as you can remember.

If you don't accept that the way you are going about your life is detrimental then nothing will change because you don't truly believe you're doing anything wrong. Why would you change something that you believe is working?

What you have read so far in this book should be all of the evidence you need to come to this realization. If you need any further proof, then consider this. You're reading this book for a reason, it's because you're not happy with the way your mind is working. You wouldn't be reading this book at all, let alone getting this far into it if the way you were thinking was correct.

Making the Change

You may be worried about changing your attitude to life because, after all, it's got you this far. You may be worried that by not letting other people's opinions effect you anymore, you may lose what you have achieved so far in life. If you do think like this, nothing will change for you. Ask yourself, do you really want things to change?

People will still offer their opinions, but hearing that opinion won't affect how you act or where you are going in life, you will only be concerned with what you truly want.

You will receive praise and validation from some people but you won't expect it or be angry when you don't get it because you don't need it. All you need is the knowledge that you are happy with what you have achieved this far.

The hard part that most people will find with this paradigm shift is that you will need to accept that it's ok for some people to have extremely negative opinions on you and even not like you at all. Or that some people will think your work is bad. You need to accept that none of this truly matters and that you can never please everyone.

Some people in this word that you cross paths with will simply not like you and it may seem unfair because they don't know you. To try and change every negative opinion you experience is impossible. So don't waste your valuable time trying to make them think otherwise.

Be Different and Stand Out

It's ok for people to not like you. It's ok to not fit the vision of the fantastic selfless human being that you see as your ideal self. It's ok to be different and not fit in with what people expect you to be.

In fact being different and standing out from the crowd is the greatest thing that you can do in my opinion. To be extraordinary and achieve greatness you need to not fit in and not appease other people.

If you stand out and if you're different, some people won't like it and they won't like you. But then again, not matter what you do there will be people who don't like you.

You need to make a simple choice. Are you really going to change yourself for them if you're doing what you really want in life? Of course not.

Your Vision and Path

When you create a goal or a set of goals that you want to achieve in life, this will set you on a path. Other people may not get it or even try to understand it. Or even if they do get it they may not agree with it or think that you're stupid for setting these goals. None of this matters.

Your parents, your partner, your co-workers, your boss, your friends, etc. They may try to discourage you if your new path doesn't fit in line with what they want from you based on their selfish desires.

Be a Visionary

This is what being a visionary is. Creating a goal and seeing it through even if other people don't believe in it. Every great visionary in history who has lived an extraordinary life would have experienced resistance on their path from other but they didn't let that stop them because they believed in their vision too much to waste time on people pleasing.

Make the Choice Today

There are two main things that can come out of this. Option one is to appease other people, get your praise and your validation by upholding your ideal self-image but sacrifice your happiness. Option two is to realize that all that truly matters is your ultimate goals in life and that people's opinions on your personal goals that have nothing to do with them are completely insignificant and above all, none of their business.

Remember Your Goal

All of this begins with setting your goal. So step one is to get a pen and paper and really get down to the root of what you want in life. I'm not talking about superficial things but the real core of what you want to achieve with your time on this earth.

If your end goal is powerful enough your path will be strong and you will be sure of it in your mind. That way when you hear opinions aimed at you, good or bad, you won't care because your belief in your path will become like a shield. All of these opinions will pale in comparison to your ultimate goal and you will realize just how insignificant and futile they are.

This is what will ultimately lead to you not caring about what people think of you.

Affirmations

If you're finding it hard to get into the mindset of not caring what other people think then affirmations can be really helpful. Affirmations work. That's why pretty much every self-help course that has ever been made recommends them. They help us to re-program our mind to accept new ideas and achieve powerful paradigm shifts.

How to Use Afirmations

An affirmation is a sentence that you repeat to yourself over and over. When said repeatedly day after day with conviction your subconscious mind will start to align to meet the affirmation.

So, the affirmation I want you to try is this, "I believe in my path in life and I will not allow the negative or positive opinions of others to hinder me."

When you say this to yourself more and more you will really start to feel the words sinking in. I want you to try this for yourself. Starting today I want you to say this affirmation to yourself for a few minutes every single day.

Believe It

Really think about what those words mean and keep your ultimate goal in your head as you say them.

You may not even notice it that strongly at first but your paradigm of automatically reacting to other people in a way that aligns with your ideal self-image will shift. Your initial reaction will not be to appease the person talking to you and seek their approval.

Reactions

People will notice this new focus in you and they may react negatively, but that's okay. You're doing this for you, not for them so it doesn't matter what they think.

This is not to say you can never appease someone again and that you will become cold hearted and never do anything nice for anyone. You can still do all of these things, but the difference is, you will be choosing to do so and not doing it because you feel expected to or in order to make them like you.

That's the aim here, is to put you on the middle path where you're not a people pleaser but you're also not a cold hearted monster. You do things for yourself and you can also choose to do things for other people if you want to.

Although as I said, at first people may not like this at first because they are used to you being a bit of a push over and they like it that way. But in the end they will actually find themselves more drawn to you because they will respect you having a backbone.

So to really get this mindset off to a great start, make sure you do your affirmations every single day. Some people find it helps to lay down and close their eyes while saying them and others prefer to look themselves in the eye in a mirror while saying them. So you can try them out and see what works best for you.

Conclusion

So to recap, we need to realize that it is our ideal self-image that is causing us to act the way we do around others. We have a paradigm in our heads that causes us to constantly try to make people see us how we see ourselves in our head. When people see us as being something other than that, we try to change their opinion. This is stressful and detrimental to our lives.

We need to also realize that we are selfish creatures and to deny that or to try and constantly be selfless and kind causes an internal struggle within us. So by people pleasing and caring about what other people think we are effectively harming ourselves.

This doesn't mean we have to become a heartless monster. We just need to find the middle ground where we can do nice things for others if we really want to, not because we feel like we have to.

We need to understand that opinions are just a figment of someone's imagination and that they can be controlled by emotions and moods. Therefore they are too random to try and control even if we try our whole lives to do so.

We also need to understand that all opinions, both good and bad, if taken to heart will change the way we act and may lead to a change in our path.

We need to accept that our current way of thinking and appeasing people isn't working for us and really believe that something needs to change.

The solution is to really find our inner desires and what we want in life. If we find our focus and clearly define our path in life, then all of the noise coming from the sidelines will seem so insignificant that it won't even matter anymore.

Final Thoughts

Well that about wraps it up for this book! I hope you enjoyed it and learned some useful information.

I have plenty of other books out about loads of topics surrounding Self Improvement and I will be putting my new books up for free trials every now and again. You can view all of my books by going to my Amazon Author page:

http://www.amazon.com/James-Umber/e/B00UXZNTB4/

Also, don't forget to go get my free book that is linked at the front of this book if you haven't already!

Thanks so much for taking an interest in my work and I hope to speak to you all again very soon!